LAMENTATIONS

Subhash Jaireth

LAMENTATIONS

For little Remi, Miles, and Hamish
and their generation

Like Calvino's Marco Polo every time I speak about a river, he says, I speak something about Solani, my river. The river doesn't belong to you, she teases. A pretence it is to believe that by calling a river my or giving it a name, one can make it acquiesce to be owned, for aren't words just sounds uttered by an anxious mind to make us feel at ease with the world, enchanting and perilous? Of course, he mumbles, and agrees that he is the one beholden to the river. To possess and be possessed is no different. They are the same just like two sides of an open palm, he confesses overawed but content. Perhaps this is the reason he can't stop calling the river his, pleading not to use the word *it* for his river because the word doesn't befit the river, alive and ever-present. You are just silly, she groans, kicks off her shoes and walks into the ankle-deep water. He watches how the river accepts her feet washing them like pebbles the river has lived for thousands of years in consonance with. There is poise in her walk, and although he knows that she knows he is watching her, he can't stop looking, enchanted by the autumn light speckled over leaves, the moist moss, weeds and the hem of her wet dress. Don't look, she calls without turning her head but he looks not at her, but at the river playing with her feet.

Tell me about the river you call Bashō's, she asks. Its real name is Mogami, he says and looks at her to see if her question is sincere or a mere trick to flatter him. *Mogami-gawa*, he repeats and writes on the paper the Kanji characters. *Samidare o atsumete haya-shi Mogami-gawa*, he reads voicing each word hesitantly like a child learning to walk. The words sound strange but pleasant, especially *haya-shi*. *Haya-shi*, she repeats silently wondering about its meaning. Gathering the rains of the wet season, she hears him speak, swift runs the Mogami River. Where is swift? She asks. *Haya-shi* (早し), he points at the characters coupled together. This is me, she says, touching the figure shaped like a hook, and the one with a hooded face is you. Definitely you, she adds and giggles. Like a hook I trap you to tease and torment, and you, as always, retreat, retract and hide. Perhaps, he says and smiles, and the smile draws a curtain over his face

•

What's more important, she asks, the river or the words Bashō wrote for it? He doesn't answer and she leaves him alone to ponder. Three days later he shows her the river on a map; his finger tracking the blue line following it all the way to the bay. *Samidare* (五月雨), he utters the word three times stressing the third syllable. It means

the summer rain, pointing the short dash lines in the third character. I see, she says. The river is swift because it gathers the fifth month rain; the rain the month of spring brings. The river rushes to return the water to the sea keeping only what it needs to be a river; to return the excess so that the sea can make the rain the following spring. Is it that simple? she wants to ask but doesn't, enchanted by the childlike certainty with which he speaks

•

For Bashō it was a river that lived in him unfettered by thoughts crowding his mind; thoughts he wanted to empty for the river to stay inside him. To look at it flow outside was like watching his mother in the garden in unison with plants, soil, and worms, and with birds, bees and butterflies; with them and yet apart. That's how the river wandered and with it the hot day too ambled dribbling into the sea. It must be the sun setting down, she says. It certainly must be, he replies with a glitter in his eyes. The shine spreads over his face that lights up like the yellow on the feathers of a goldfinch. The source of his joy, she muses, is her innate ability to guess the thought taking shape in his mind. The people who love Bashō, he says, call the river Bashō's. Going to the river for them is akin to going to meet the poet, who walked to write and wrote to walk

to every new mountain, river, or grove. Like water in a river, she hears herself mumble, amazed that the words which should have come from him have found her instead.

Let me tell you about Abe-e Rokni, the water-of-Rokni, of Hafez, he says. She waits but he doesn't know where to start; from the river which isn't quite a river or from Hafez, the poet, who imagined himself to be the bulbul of Shiraz whose songs are heard everywhere. She enjoys seeing him wedged, unable to find words he thinks are always kind to him; they come to him slow but assured, almost like the flow in a meandering river pirouetting with the banks. The water in Abe-e Rokni, he speaks after a pause, is warm in winters and cold in summers. This is because the river which isn't a river, is blind, hidden from the light of the sun, the moon and the stars. It is sweeter than any *aragh-e bahar narenji*, the orange-blossom water sold in the bazaars of Shiraz; and it's more winy than any wine in *bihisht*, the paradise. The righteous are promised in the afterlife. Shiraz was the paradise Hafez pined for, although he hardly ever left the city nestled in a narrow valley boiling hot in the summer and icy-cold in the winter. 'Even in Shiraz,' he speaks, he fancies Hafez saying, 'I miss Shiraz when I watch *anar*, the pomegranate tree, in blossom.' Here comes Bashō again, she thinks and smiles imagining like him, the two, Hafez and Bashō, engaged in silent tête-à-tête

•

Karizgars, they are called, he says. Not dowsers but lovers of water, they know how to read memories the water carries, and therefore the future it awaits. The water trusts them because they sing chants and hymns before making a request or a petition. The *karizgars* saw the water seep through the cracks in the limestone and asked if it would like to leave the dark cavern to enjoy once again the delights of the world under the sky. It yielded, he says, and became Abe-e Rokni, she adds finishing his phrase. He smiles glad how her imagination runs ahead of his words light and swift like Cheshmeh Chenar, the spring the *karizgars* had seen in the mountains. They planted a row of chinars to give the young water a screen from the blinding sun. The water liked the chinars especially in the autumn when they are lit up bright like fire, he says and pauses to look at her, his eyes fixed on her lush auburn hair. Like you, she waits to hear but he has water on his mind. The *karizgars* dug trenches underground lining them with brick, lime and mortar and the water liked what it saw and went inside to flow and rise wherever it was asked. It filled the pools and ponds in the gardens one of which is Golgast-e Mosalla, the Garden of Mosalla, the one Hafez loved more than the garden in paradise he wasn't keen to step inside

•

I want to go to Golgast-e Mosalla, he says. To see Cheshmeh Chenar? she asks. No, he says, but to visit Hafeziyeh, the Tomb of Hafez, and to sit by his dust with wine and music. But you don't drink, she says. You do, he replies and looks at her. She smiles at the manner he has asked her to come with him to Shiraz. He describes the garden, its orange grove, chinars, and slender cypresses. Are there any *anars*, the pomegranates? she asks. There must be, he says and shows her a picture of the grave topped by a marble stone calligraphed with verses of a ghazal. Above the grave rises a copper dome, shaped like the hat of a dervish. We'll touch the marble stone with both hands, he says, and read silently the verses in the three languages I know. She notices the shift from 'I' to 'we' and resents how easily he has assumed that she would join him in the ritual he wants to enact. Go on, she says. We'll find a man, he replies, holding a leather bag with coloured cards and a goldfinch perched on his shoulder. The bird will land on the bag and pick a card for him to read the verse. And? she asks. In it will be the clue, he says, to answer the question I want to ask you. Why don't you ask me now? she wants to say bemused, but doesn't because she knows he wants to continue the game. We'll come out of the garden, he says and walk the street under

which flows Abe-e Rokni in the *kariz*, pretending we can hear the water. You mean all the way? she asks. No, he says but a few hundred steps and then go to the mountain to find Cheshmeh Chenar. And sit with the chinars, she adds. Of course, he says. In the autumn? she asks again. Certainly, he says ending the game for now.

Like Borges's Youwarkee, he says, a woman who is also a bird, the lake is half lake and half river, a river that has become a lake and a lake that doesn't want to forget that it is a river. Like Piccinini's *The Skywhale*, she intervenes, a whale that wants to fly as a bird showing off its pendulous breasts, profuse, fecund, and generous, very much like a meandering river you adore. O yes, he says, yes, and smiles; a smile she remembers that lit up his sad face, seeing the creature take off in the sea-sky. It floated at first ponderous, and then lifted by the wind, rose high above the water. Go, she heard him whisper. Go, she herself murmured, and it glided in the sky and in the lake, for the sky was in the lake, and the lake held the creature in the crook of its ruffled arm. In the autumn sun the breasts glowed like amber swaying off its malachite back, and the gracious wind nudged it to turn its face for them to look, and they looked. It's glorious, she said. And sad, he responded. Like you, she wanted to say but was distracted by a couple rowing a canoe, oblivious of the wondrous creature that had made the lake graceful and the sky benevolent. That's when they heard a pair of crimson rosellas on the stringybark behind their back call: the two-tone piping whistles propping and sparring each other

•

The name we call the lake by, he says, hides in it whispers of other names. Like seams in lithified sand, she adds, imitating his encultured voice, that holds in it ripples, fossils, and concretions. Yes, he says with a stutter, unsure if he should ignore her teasing, goading voice, but he does, and soon the stutter is replaced by a measured flow, akin to the water in the creek they had walked across a few hours before. The river the lake is nourished by, he continues sidestepping her barely audible groan, is called Yeal-am bidgee by the Moolinggolah before it meanders into the Limestone Plains. Moolinggolah, she whispers to herself, and wants him to utter the four-syllable word again, enchanted by the rounded 'oos' which sound like polished pebbles prattling with the river indulgent like his grandmother he calls Dadima. The name Molonglo is purloined, fashioned from Moolinggolah, the word that fills our mouth like a ripened plum. He speaks trying to keep the saliva from dripping, and she smiles. For the Ngambri, the river is Ngambri too, as is the wombat mountain which holds in between its paws the river and the lake. The place, the river, and the people have the same name, for they exist together from the deepest of times, knitted like strands in the tapestry of the wondrous world. He loves the round sounds and

shapes, she hears her mind whisper, and a little tickling tingle runs down her spine

•

She holds in her hand a piece of rock rounded at the edges. Kissed by the river, he calls it. The grey rock with corals and shells, and cracks and cavities, one of which is filled with yellow-brown clay that stains her hand. It's a limestone, isn't it? she says. I found it behind a cottage a week ago jogging around the lake. Yes, it is, he says holding the rock cupped in his hands then raising the blessed piece to his right ear. To hear the waves of the warm ancient sea, she imagines, lapping the shore. Listen, he says returning her the rock which she brings close to her ear bearing a hematite stud. And she hears not waves but the riffle of water in a sedate satisfied river. It's a river I hear, she says. Yes, the same Ngambri hobnobbing with the lithified ooze, millions of years old. So, the river lives, she says, deep underneath the lake. It does, it does, he says, the river and the valley filled with sand and gravel and marked by the footprints of the Ngambri. They were in the river and the river was in them, and the two were in the river in the sky that kept watch on them when they slept and dreamed. To the river they came to fish and forage, and in the sand on the dunes and ridges they left their tools, spears and pestles. And their

coolamons perhaps, she adds. They found caves in the limestone the river had carved where they sheltered painting on the wall and the roof plants and animals, stars and skies, wind and sand, and the river itself, she says finishing his phrase. He listens and then after a pause touches her hand wrapped around the rock and kisses her ringless fingers, and just for a moment she feels as if she holds in her hand the curls of time crumpled like a handkerchief

•

It is written not merely by light but by the lake itself: the photo in which rounded granite boulders stand barefoot in the lake like some primeval Elders, the holders of law and lore, placating with their chants and clapsticks the spirit of the world. Let's go there, she says, to the rocks and the water in the photo to celebrate the friendship between the two and to hail Budjabulya, the serpent the Ngunnawal believe created the rock, the river, the lake, and all the living creatures including themselves. And thus, they stand one late afternoon in the winter stalked by the wind turbines perched on the spine of stubby hills with sunshine bouncing off the grey and pink granites speckled with iridescent mica flakes. The winter day is dry and cold, and the lake, parched following the hot summer and autumn, has called the water home to take

refuge in dips and dints, holes and hollows, rimmed with tusks of grass, hushed by the frost. The granites stand marooned, like the boat, he says, he once saw in the Aral Sea, near the mouth of Amu Darya starved of water. They stroke and scan the rocks, counting marks the water had left when the lake would have brimmed and bounced around them. The rocks don't forget, he says, the lake's embrace. Neither does the lake, she adds, because they both give and receive and thereby partake a measure of each other. The giving enriches them, and the lake shares its portion of the rocks with sand, soil, and clay, with plants, animals, and people, and with the wind. The rocks and the lake thus disperse into the wetness that surrounds the earth like amniotic fluid. He listens and nods as they sit down on the sand to watch a blue-tongue lizard sunning on one of the boulders. It yawns and flicks its tongue, but the hiss soon drowns in the wind weaving chords of sounds in the silence, pristine, almost primordial. Blessed they feel being with the rocks and the lake and with each other. We'll come again, hopes one of them. Perhaps, the other

muses

•

Let's go to the rocks and the lake again, she says, not to see but to hear the rain talking to them. He isn't surprised by the invitation,

for he knows how attuned her ears are to the sounds our bodies make. Even dead the body emits sounds, he has heard her say, not noise but sound, as it disperses to confuse with dust and water. She utters the word stressing the sound *fuse* and he realises how it cleaves the word open to hear the intonations, hidden at first, clear and salient. They stand with the granites, shin-deep in water, listening to the drizzle dint and dent the watery skin of the lake which responds with a pizzicato played on a cello. The wind picks up the chords and carries the glissando past the rocks which crackle and sputter. She takes off her shoes and socks to walk in the lake. He doesn't follow her but leaning against one of the rocks hears her turn into an instrument played on by the water, the wind, the weeds, and the mud. They play on her, and she on them, her feet, her arms, her head, her whole glorious self. And then she disappears in the mist, but the sounds persist. She is there, she is there, his mind whispers and when she reappears, followed by a rumble of thunder, he drops all desire to describe her and the rocks and the lake. Let it go, he says, let it go, and his mind relents seduced by the word *later*. But later will never arrive. The rain, the rocks, and the lake brimming with water, will remain un-worded, unhooked, unhinged, and perhaps thereby pristine. There isn't any

need to talk, he'll imagine hearing her say
and he would resist even to say 'yes'

•

Underneath the water in the lake there are other waters, he says, ancient and young at the same time. The water is ageless, for it shares the strings of time with whatever it touches and is touched by. Now he is going to show me a map, she thinks, because for him without a map the real remains ephemeral like a kiss that needs the touch of skin to become a kiss. Look, he says, spreading before her his left hand cupped to make a dint in the middle. This is the lake the Ngambri call Weereewa, the dark water. For the Ngunnawal it is Ngungara, the flat one. It is flat when filled with water, thin like a film, and dark when the water goes underground. He asks her to place her index finger touching the tip of his thumb. There is a fissure here, he says, along which the rocks were pushed to form a hollow for the lake to fill. This is where Budjabulya, the serpent, rests, she says. He does, he replies, keeping watch on the wind, the clouds and the skies. When he sings, the Ngambri believe, the skies rejoice calling in the rain clouds. Then the creeks flounce and flow, he says, pointing lines on his palm, rushing to wash the clayey skin of the lake. What the lake cannot hold, seeps into the sand and gravel below to take its place in the

pores and cracks. There it lives exchanging wetness with the dry clay, scorched by the sun and blustered by the wind. Wait, she says, imitating the witter of dark water, wait, for the rain will surely come. He listens cradled as if by the lullaby-sounds she makes, and the dent in his cupped hand feels warm and moist reminding him of his mother's neck, nestled against which he slept dreaming of rivers and lakes years and years ago.

This is for you, she says, showing him a plant in a large pot. Really? he asks. Of course, she says. Gymea lily? he enquires with a stutter in his voice. What else? she says. Now you have to find the right place for it to grow and blossom. I already have, he says. She is surprised not by his reply but by the quickness with which he reclaims control of his emotions. No chink, no crack, no flaws; solid as the malachite pot, and ready to tell stories he knows she likes. There is a story, he says, that D'harawal, the Cabbage Palm people, tell. The story of Kai'mia, the ancient young warrior who lived near the waters of Kai'eemah, the river draining into a bay, that Captain Cook named the Botany Bay. And he stops. She waits. He looks at the leaves, his right hand caressing their fibrous silky shine. I can't tell his story, he speaks, still staring at the plant, as if it wasn't just a plant. To tell it I have to belong, and belong I can't, for each time I tell the story to myself, I confront the face of an imposter gazing at me in the mirror. The lasso of stories, he adds, I cast to snare life with returns to me each time

bare, barren, bereft

•

Three days later he hands her a book to read. It has the story he didn't want to tell the other day. Garuwanga, the D'harawal call it, she says reading aloud the title. He

repeats the word as if he has heard it for the first time. Gunyalungalung, she utters the second word she has found in the glossary. He tries but trips each time on the third syllable of the Dharug word. She asks him to listen again and repeat and he tries unable to harness the sound. He will sulk for days now, she thinks, not because he has been upstaged by a novice, but because the childish delight with which he finds new things for her has been robbed. It took me hours, she says, to feel its presence in my mouth, and it sounded like water rippling past the moist pebbles. She looks at him, soft and pliant, chastened as if by her will to be assertive, and this saddens her just a little

•

Up in the mountains in the swamp spread over the sandstones, there are creeks, he says, one of which turns into Kai'eemah after traversing kilometres, gathering water from springs, streams, and creeks. There, near the swamp in the shadow of the stringybarks I saw three Gymea lilies in their primeval floral glory. The blood-red trumpet crowning the tall pale green spike sparkled like a Japanese lantern setting aglow the evening air. I looked and looked, he says, like I look at you, she imagines him say, but he stops stranded as if the words he is searching for don't exist. The relief arrives in the form of a seed pod, crusty

brown, ovalene and with a gaping mouth revealing yellowing crispy seeds. He places the pod in her palm and waits for her to speak. It's warm, she wants to say, like the squab of a crested pigeon she had found a year ago, fallen out of a nest on the hakea in her back garden. Like the bird the pod feels

alive ready to shoot out

•

It is just three-steps wide, he says, the stream, as it descends from the swamp filling the narrow creek lined with stringybarks and scribbly gums. The summer day was hot and the water sluggish, unwilling to drown the gravelly riffles and content to find its way around them. I watched a pair of king parrots perched on the fallen trunk of a stringybark, the female boisterous trying to push her companion off, he says and smiles. And the lyrebird? she asks. The lyrebird didn't call. Bad luck, she says. Because you weren't there, she imagines him say, and rebukes the silly thought hopping in her mind. But I saw two white-throated treecreepers spiral up the stringybark ignoring a drowsy koala wedged safely inside the crook of the tree's elbow. Quiet it was, so quiet that I heard a twig whisper in the air as it floated and dropped in the water not far from the trunk. The parrots took off followed by the treecreepers, but the koala just opened his eyes, wiggled and went back

to sleep after a few reluctant snorts. Why did the twig fall? he asks. To let you feel the quietness of the quiet, she replies

•

A few steps from the bridge, he says, the river forms a pool before cascading down the sandstones. The water is below knee-high and the flow unhurried. It began to rain as I walked in the water. The autumn drizzle soft and light, as if taking care not to hit and hurt the water. I sat in the water on a moss-covered rock surrounded by lush verdure of stringybarks, gums, wattles and casuarinas searching for … Gymea lily, she says interrupting the flow. Yes, he says, because it grows in the hollow of bloodied footprints Kai'mia, the young warrior, left on the D'harawal land. I am not good at spotting plants, he confesses, and feel at home with rocks, sand and mud. I know, she says, as he passes her two pebbles of quartz he had found dislodged from the sandstone at the base of the first cascade. The smaller of the two is a perfect egg, light blue, and waxy. I washed it, he says, and put it in my mouth feeling its curves with my tongue. Should I try? she wonders but is distracted by the rough, sharp edges of the second piece. They are old, he says, millions of years, older than the sandstone in which they sit. And they could have come from rocks which now lie under the snow and

ice of Antarctica, he says and looks to see if she finds the fact fascinating. She does but keeps quiet and this quietens him too

•

Like Roger Deakin, he says, I want to swim with the river as it flows into the sea. He loves *Waterlog*, and Deakin's insatiable desire to swim in the rivers and creeks of his land. It won't be safe, she says, for they are aware of the toxic plumes carried by the groundwater seeping into the river. For weeks he surveys the maps, makes enquiries, and gives up. And you aren't a good swimmer, she tells him to dampen the disappointment. I know, he says but my awkward breaststroke is good enough to negotiate fifty or so metres. I'm not sure, she wants to warn, but shows him instead an aerial photo of the bay near the river mouth. See, she whispers, how the waters mix: the cafe-latte of the river streaking through the celadon-green of the sea. Malachite-green, he corrects her, and there, a little further, the topaz-blue. But his excitement is fleetingly brief, and looking, as if for reassurance, he lets his dark brown hand linger for more than a moment on her pale hand. Always cold, her mind whispers, as the warmish quiver of his palm and fingers runs through her like a sip of fresh lemon and ginger tea they had together an hour earlier. She waits for him to pull his hand away, but he

doesn't and she lets the moment endure a little longer. To touch and be touched is what the water invites, he'll tell her later. Seeing is only a counterfeit, enchanting but deficient. Words, she'll think listening to him, can't always hide or contain the swell of desire that the body feels and unwittingly reveals

•

Goolay'yari, he says, the D'harawal call a pelican, he says, looking at the sign which reads Pelican Point. Goolay'yari is also the name of the river which used to run past here, thousands of years ago, and join Kai'eemah. She looks following his finger tracing the ancient river's flow under the waters of the bay. The early morning sun is soft, the air misty with salty spray, and the sand pliant and crunchy underfoot. They walk tracking the drowned valleys, the sand and gravel of which might still remember the watery touch as might the twigs, leaves, pollen and the fossil shells and bones, and … the fishhooks, she hears herself speak. Of course, he says, and the footprints of people who would have walked, run and danced. Look, she says, as a pair of eastern curlew land in the muddy sand. The pink on the long black bill glimmers. The male wavers and wobbles behind, hesitant, uninterested. Its mournful *karr-er* drowned by the bubbling high-pitched *kerlee-kerlee* of the

female. A nice pair, you two, she thinks as she watches him walk past them eager to reach the sandspit

•

She is surprised by the ease with which they find the right rhythm to paddle the kayak, because when they walk, they are always out of step; she swift and hasty, and he sombre and ponderous. He would, no doubt, credit the underground river flowing beneath, but for her the joy of the moment is innate and therefore would remain unreasoned, unexplained. Meanwhile the kayak glides on the shallow water, handling the waves with skill but without flourish or arrogance. The sea is calm, the light soothes, and the motion mesmerises asking the body to acquiesce. And acquiesce she does, enchanted by the shimmer of mica, quartz and rusty oxides in the sand on the spit. Behind her back she hears him breathe and wishes she had a rear-view mirror to look at his unwary face, blessing and blessed. He must be searching for Gymea lily, she thinks, well aware that to find it here in the mangroves, saltmarshes and the dune woodland would be a miracle. Yes, a miracle, she hears him say, not surprised that he has ensnared the whispered thought. And at that very moment, as if to celebrate the event, a young ruddy turnstone lands on the kayak,

eager to balance itself on its short orange legs. The reddish-brown band on its breast sparks in the light as it looks at her bemused. The exchange between them is brief for the bird soon issues a quick rattle and takes off

carried away by the playful wind

•

Like sand grains in the drowned river valleys, he says, which preserve the impressions of water, words retain the memory of lost languages. To walk on the ground underneath which flow the ancient rivers, for him, is to mourn the loss of rivers and languages. Each D'harawal word he utters, he explains, is a pebble of hope he feels carrying in his mouth; hope that one day D'harawal songs and stories would begin to flow again like daragun, the water creeks. For the D'harawal, gadu is the sea lapping the shoreline, and garrigarrang, the one that spreads beyond the breaking waves where gawura, the humpback whales come to frolic in the season of Wirtijirbin, the superb lyrebird. Dugongs used to visit as well but the D'harawal word for them has been lost. The water in the present-day bay is cold for dugongs, but eight thousand years ago when the warm sea began to rise and turned the fresh water daragun into estuaries, they came looking for sea grasses in the brackish water. One of them lost its way, beached and perished. The people

saw it breathe its last; an old woman raised her arms and wailed; the rest joined her to step-dance around her, chanting words of grief and gratitude, wishing its spirit a safe passage to the other world, guarded by Bilima, the long-necked turtle. It left its bones, found fossilised in the river sediments next to the remains of pollen and plants, of roots, stumps and peat. We walked past the site last year, he says; the site not far from which now stands the florist shop where we bought for your grandma a bouquet of banksias, and boronia roses of two different colours

•

It could have happened somewhere here, he says, seated on a mossy rock, washed by the waters of Wollondilly, pattering with pebbles. Like now, he says, sun was about to go down; his words briefly interrupted by the crackle of kookaburras, perched on the leafless branch of a tall bai'yali, the stringy bark. Barragula, they call it, the time of the fading day when the food needs to be cooked and fed. The day was wet, and the night would be cold like it always is in the final days in the season of Marrai'gang, the autumn. The sound of the first shots were drowned by the cries of garral, the black cockatoos. Boo'dhawaa, the owls, shrieked, and the quolls squealed. The people ran to escape or hide, slipped and rolled down the

cliffs to land on the slippery rocks. Death came slowly but surely, and left the bodies near the waters of Wollondilly, unmourned. But the river still mourns, he says, for they believe that Wollondilly is the place where the spirits of the dead dwell. Like a river, the dead don't die, they just dissolve, shedding their presence in the water, the sand, the grass and on the mossy rock, fissured and flaked by time. The river keeps them stowed for us to rummage, remember, and grieve. And that's when we hear, she speaks, urged by a force unbeknown to her, the shots, the cries and the sound of scared feet running. They sit together, breathing quietly, waiting for something to happen, looking as if for a sign that their presence has been noticed and felt, but nothing happens. Soon they get up to walk away when they hear the whipping call of a bird. They turn to look. An eastern whipbird, she says. The bird calls again then stops. That's that, he says breaking the silence. Not quite, she replies.

They are like arteries and veins, he says, looking at the map she shows him; a map she bought online, hoping that it would drag him out of the stupor he seems to have been marooned in for days. She doesn't know the reason and to speculate about it is futile and pointless. Sadness suits him, for when he is sad he offers a smile like an apology, hesitant but honest. You don't have to, she wants to say; you are sad because there is too much sorrow in the world but the grief he feels, she knows, is for rivers who have lost the river-ness, their way of being a river. A dead river is still a river, she wants to retrieve the words he had once lent to her; the words burrowed in her mindscape like valleys: present, past, and possibly future. Why possibly? She knows he would whisper not in his meandering, sedate voice of the timbre of a baritone saxophone, but with his dark and dreary eyes, now beginning to mislay the glint that once upon a time nestled in them. Then, years ago, the glimmer speckled like light bouncing off the water in a river; there is a river inside me, the eyes, she thought, said. To be kissed they asked for, not the eyes but the light, serene but often playful and impish. To have him as a child growing inside her, that's what she could have felt. You are strange, she remembers scolding her frolicsome mind, but she is glad that it

hasn't misplaced the image, wondrous and
uncanny at the same time

•

Tell me about veins and arteries, he asks. Don't they string through us like creeks and rivers; our body a landscape nourished by them? Yes, she says, yes, surprised how suddenly the scientist in her rushes out with words which he would festoon with metaphors arranged to the rhythm of feet ready to be read as chants. To celebrate and grieve is his purpose, and she, the interlocutor, walking arm in arm with his and her own words, a celebrant as well as a mourner. Yes, she says, they run for thousands of kilometres in our bodies just over a metre tall, crisscrossing like fibres of a fishnet. Hundreds of Volgas, and Gangas, he adds, and perhaps more. Yes, she says, and they carry with them oxygen stitched loosely to iron that makes the blood haematitic red. She utters the three syllables with care, releasing the sound, caressed by her moist tongue and lips which enter his ears and wet him from head to toe. I like haematite, he says, the word, the mineral, and the colour it stains everything it touches with. The blood in the fish, snakes and goannas, she says, isn't red but bluish, for it is copper on which the oxygen piggybacks. Copper, he repeats, his eyes fixed on the azurite bracelet he had

bought for her in a flea market in Nicosia, a gift of the river Pedieos, carried down from the heights of the Troodos Mountains. She watches him stare and feels his gaze reach the skin underneath and the blood in her veins quickens. The revelation that follows is sudden and sombre: there is a river of stories that meanders between them, the stories they'll whisper to the son or daughter they would have or perhaps not.

What do you think? he asks. It looks like a kangaroo, she says, of the tail-like shape in the photo. The Thirrari call this lake Kati Thanda, he says, the skin of a primal animal stretched over the lands. Once spread, it also becomes the skin of the landscape; the two wrapped together holding each other and everything else, real and imagined. It's the skin, she says, that lets them breathe in unison, nourishing one another. It's the skin, he continues, we touch, when we walk, sit, stand or sleep. It's the skin, she adds, that receives us once we die embracing our remains, and it's the skin through which we share our memory of the world that endures without us and yet with us. It was the skin of the animal, he remembers, the young Thirrari boy carried over his head to drape the country of his ancestors. There is a little hill, he says, pointing at a spot on the photo, where the Thirrari believe the boy took shelter and continues its presence uninterrupted. They call the hill Dúturúnna. Perhaps he is the one, she imagines, who calls in the rain; the rain that falls in the uplands far, so far away, waited patiently by creeks and rivers which bring it to the lake. Maybe he is, he responds, relishing the way her voice seeks to capture the farness from where the water makes its lumbering way. Her voice embellished by an image his fanciful mind

of its own will creates; there she is, standing on the glistening white saltpan, her arms stretched wide in the endless space. Isn't she beautiful, his mind prods him to say but

he doesn't

•

Aren't they granites? she asks. They certainly are, he replies, millions of years old, carrying on their skin marks of rust left by air, water, wind, and whirling sand dust. That's why they are red, she says. Yes, but only the skin, the flesh it covers is either pink or grey. The Arabana and the Wangkangurru call the boulders Thanti-wanparda, because of the story ingrained in them; and the story is of Minparu, an old rainmaker, and his grandson. That appears to be his head, she says, looking at the photo, and on his shoulders he carries the little boy. The two stand on the banks of the creek which is accustomed to waiting for the water because it is infrequent but when it arrives, it unleashes torrents, brief but full of promise. The clouds often fly past like eaglehawks, so high in the sky that the heat keeps the water warmer than the dew point. Next year perhaps, Minparu, the clever man of the desert, whispers to himself, and to the wind which hears his murmurs, as it traces rapid pirouettes with the dust scattered on the hot stones of the rocky desert. No need to waste words. No need at all, the

wind seems to repeat the words sputtering searing grainy noises in agreement. The old man hasn't forgotten how fussy and fickle the clouds are and therefore values patience more than anger or insolence. The clouds will relent, he knows, as they always do, and then his chants with gypsum, the rain stone, in his hand will work their magic. He sounds like my opa, she says, who spoke less but always with purpose. The words ignore the profligate like me, he replies with a tinge of sadness in his voice that she is keen to keep safe inside the nooks and crannies of her prodigious memory: a rare memento for her son or daughter who remain at that moment just a nascent idea in her quirky mind

•

There is Warrana, the whirlwind, the Arabana believe lives on an island in the lake; he appears when the lake is dry covered by a honeycomb crust of salt. He sings to invite the wind which arrives and they twist, twirl, and spin together. The sand and flakes of salt rise in the dusty funnel of the whirlwind grabbing whatever comes in their way: yuri-yuri, the lizard, wabma, the snake, and even malda-yapa, the little dingoes. It's better to keep out of his way for his fury is unfettered and his hunger insatiable. The Arabana call him Windi-pilpa, the eyebrows, because that's what you see when you dare to look;

just eyebrows and nothing more. And he wheezes and whistles, splutters and snorts, and his eyebrows twitch and tremble. He is angry, very angry, people watching from over the mounds tell each other and look for songs to pacify his rage and to make him disappear in his dark and dusty hole. Eyebrows, she imagines, thick like the tail of the brushtail possum that lives on the scribbly gum in her garden and turns noisier on nights aglow with a full moon:

large, happy, and always flirtatious

•

When the lake is dry, and the creeks littered with gravel and red-hot pebbles lodged in the lumps of desiccated clay, there is water in the rivers underneath nestled in the lithified sand deposited in an ancient sea millions of years ago. It is a precious gift conferred by the clouds which are set afloat over the highlands thousands of kilometres away. It is ageless, for each year the ancient water is replenished by fresh rain, and the two trickle together through the pores and pits in the sandstones unhurried, traversing a metre or two each year and sharing with the rocks whatever they are ready to give and accept. But it must be salty, she murmurs, because of the slow pace and the prolonged embrace with minerals and fossils. Yes, it is, almost as salty as the sea you love to swim, ski, and paddle in. And it's lukewarm

like fresh milk from one of your mother's gracious cows you call Masha. Dasha, she recalls the name of the cow's twin wishing to go home to see them and her mother. The water too remembers the ocean from where it has come and to which it longs to return, he says. Hence, it rises hundreds of metres up the cracks sucked as if by a straw in a bottle of soda-water filling holes and hollows forming mounds of salts around springs, soaks, and sprouts. Ngurabana, the Arabana call their country sprinkled with bubblers, a treasured offering of their ancestral spirits linked by the songlines mapped by them on the land and in their heart and mind. Like the sun, water is life, they say; without water no dreams, no stories, no songs or dances. Without water there is no joy, hope or wonder, he announces and looks at her as if she is one of the mikiri, the eternal spring, the source of life and living, and the luminous thought fills her with delight

•

It's sad, he says, to watch a river disappear in the sand and stones of a desert without even a whimper. But does it really disappear? she challenges and that shakes him out of his unusual reticence. No, it doesn't, he says after a pause, trying to find a string to thread words of hope and assurance. It's only the water that moves out of sight because the

river remains alive, tattooed on the skin, flesh, and bones of all the animated and the in-animated with which it has shared its riverness. To adapt and change is its nature. Isn't that right? he asks seeking affirmation and approval like a child from a mother. She enjoys this moment of doubt and hesitance. It isn't going to last, she is certain, because he will soon like the Finke River, he wants to tell her about, overflow swirling with ideas and revelations and his words will rediscover the meandering bed of steady and sumptuous imagination

•

The Arrernte call it Lara Beinta, the salt river, he says because when it isn't a river, it is content to become a gathering of water- and boggy-holes, a little salty to drink but not unpleasant to swim in. It was different eons ago when it rushed keen to bequeath its load into a large ocean in the east. Upstream in the ranges where it begins its timid steps now, the riverbed still bears traces of its ancient past. And it also preserves the memory of its life with Kati Thanda that began thousands of years ago. Then the lake was a sea expansive and fecund, and the river was pleased to play its role. These days the sea has receded, pushed back by the desert that welcomes the river, a dear old relative. Isn't the desert a sea as well? she asks, a sea of red haematitic stones

and buff and orange ridges of sand dotted with clumps of spinifex and little turrets of termite mounds. Yes, it is, he says. A desert-sea where life spurts and trickles, busier often in the coolness of either a starry sky or a majestic desert moon. The wind blows shifting sand from one crest to another, playing rhapsodic melodies as if on organs, which appear to float like sailboats on the desert waves. Now he'll recall Bach, she imagines. Without Bach nothing for him is complete and meaningful. But he doesn't and in the silence, she hears the old and wise Minparu sing: The wind whirls on Kati Thanda/ the wind swirls/ it doesn't stop/ it doesn't, up there, not far, not far.

To know a river, one has to go to its source, he says. Are you sure? she asks, thinking that he has erred, misled perhaps by the arrogance that Bashō would have made fun of. I am sorry, he says after a prolonged silence. The source of a river is water of diverse beginnings, and once it has fashioned itself into a river its purpose is to return to the wetness that engulfs the planet. The urge to search for the origin is an illusion for no one knows when or where anything begins or ends; flow and flux is what the world is made of, and togetherness, however joyous or torturous, is our predicament. Why predicament? she dares to test him again but abandons the urge, an act of arrogance itself, because she is certain that he will soon begin to question the sureness tainting his views and beliefs. Like water in a river his thoughts are a blend of currents and counter-currents. To question everything including the question itself is what fascinates him most

•

Whanganui is a stream of tears shed by the sky-father, Ngati Hau, the people of the river, believe, he says. The tears fell on the foot of Ruapehu which stands alone, rising above the clouds reaching heights unfathomed except by gods. The sky-father watched the river with delight as it rushed along narrow ravines and descended into the flatter

terrain arrayed with ridges and mounds and lush podocarpus forest, fashioning through them a drapery of graceful bends. Go, he said to the river, for the mighty sea waits for you. And then to make its passage smooth and faultless he entreated taniwha, the guardian spirits, to reside at the bends, to ensure that at the bends the river is most affectionate, generous, and acquiescent, eager to share itself with all the entities of the world it finds ready to give and receive. Without the river they are forsaken as is the river without them. Together they spread seeds of life to flourish. Together they make the world opulent, bursting with vitality. To exist with and for each other is the hymn they sing together, which pleases the sky-father beyond any measure. '*Ko au te awa, ko te awa ko au*' ('I am the river and the river is me'), she says, recalling the words of her ageless granduncle, the brother of her grandmother. He listens and repeats the Māori words and slowly tears begin to trickle from his eyes. She wants to raise her hand to touch but he turns his face away leaving her stranded for a moment or two, after which he looks at her again; his face serene, his eyes ebullient, radiating hope and confidence

•

Te Awa Tupua, Ngati Hau say about Whanganui, the river which like *te taura whiri*, the plaited rope, binds together the world around it. Te Awa Tupua, they say because the river is Tupuna, the ancestor, the bearer of knowledge and law. Te Awa Tupua, they say because it is *mauri*, their life force and hence sacred. Te Awa Tupua, they say, for they entwine with it as soon as they seed and grow inside their mothers. Te Awa Tupua, they chant because it embodies the living wholeness with the world. Te Awa Tupua, they say because the river speaks and asks us to listen and hear, and to heed and respond. Te Awa Tupua, they say to remind us that they are many others like Whanganui on our planet and perhaps far beyond

•

Instead of the skyline track running close to the top of the ridge they decide to walk along the grassy oxbow in the valley formed by the ancient channel of Whanganui girdling around Puketapu, a hill shaped like a large comma punctuating the landscape. Which way, he asks, clockwise or anti-clock? Clockwise, of course, she replies without hesitation. He is pleased for this means that they would trace the flow of Whanganui when it was happy to remain inside the luxurious loop it had carved thousands of years ago. It abandoned the meandering

bend to appease the torrents of water caused by an incessant deluge upstream forcing the river to cut a short passage, straight at first but modified later into a narrow hook. They tread single file, she ahead and he, like a lugubrious turtle, a few steps behind, forcing her to stop and look back. That must be the old channel, she says, pointing at the creek lined by patches of trees coiling through the lush verdure of grassland. He nods in agreement and hands her an oblong reddish-brown pebble with a flattened top. It's from the shales, he says, clinched and cuddled by Whanganui years and years ago. It's warm and soft like an egg, its touch reassuring. She wants to hand it back to him when they hear the insistent calls of a pair of cuckoos concealed in the canopy of beeches dotting the slope of Puketapu. They look around and are charmed by a large eagle in the pristine sky; the unfettered, flawless flight, buoyed by warm air. The afternoon light pleases, its glow gratifies and in the impeccable silence they hear the patient riffle of water in the channel. Perfect, his mind whispers. Immaculate, her mind is keen to respond.

They are painted by the river, he says, showing her the catalogue of canvases hung on the stony walls of a granite fort sinking slowly in the mud of the estuary. And by the sea, she adds. Very true, he agrees because the rhythmic pulse of the river is choreographed by tides, synchronised with the moon waxing and waning. But the real painting is the coastal landscape itself. A self-portrait isn't it? she asks. Indeed, he says, and to support her intriguing thought unfolds a coloured map of the Medway Estuary and its mud-green branches spread out like that of a tree splitting and stitching islands and marshlands, the sinews of a living wholeness that came into being thousands of years ago and will surely outlive us, the sapiens, the so-called wisest of the wise. The canvases displayed on the walls are the facsimiles of nature's self-portrait, validating that it exists in itself, and for itself, with and without us. Now I am lost, she wants to say a touch irritated by his attempts to appear profound, but she is impressed by the painterly map, with its palette dominated by verdigris strewn with splashes of greyish and brownish mud

•

First the tarpaulin canvases were laid down, he explains, spreadeagle on the muddy bed of the estuary and tethered with wooden pegs. The tide was low, but the sea water

swelled when it rose ushering surges upstream. With each pulse of the tide, it laid down, like brush strokes, slivers of silt, dotted with odd shells, and stray strands of weed on the canvases that stretched and strained, pushed and pulled by the waves. For days and nights of one lunar cycle the water went up and down the canvases which felt its touch and heard its sounds, adding their own to the polyphony composed and played by the water, wind, and the rain. In between the tides, gulls, terns and plovers ventured out to feed and hopped across the canvases engraving their toe prints. A few feathers fell off and floated and were caught in the mud on the sheets. The wind found a stray plastic wrapper of a chocolate bar and carried it around till it was trapped by the salty marsh mud. As were the fragments of peat and drops of diesel from a barge chugging past. Just after the first night of the new cycle, the canvases were retrieved and carried to be dried, looked at and touched here and there by the painter's reluctant and gentle brush. Now they were ready to be hung on the walls of the fort, for the viewers. They arrived in boats to gaze at the estuary's magical touch and wonder if they too were nothing but minor details on

nature's painted landscape

•

In the early spring of the first year of the new millennium, he says, people welcomed the river inside an old church near the dockyards. It didn't come alone but brought with it memories of the last and the first high tides of the old and new year. Memories painted by it and the sea on canvases hung across the windows like muddy stained-glass. People who came for the audience were greeted by sunlight pouring from behind the windows, setting aglow a halo around the canvases as if they were ikons attesting the otherworldly presence of the estuary, exuding uncanny power to charm and bless. Is this the same river we know intimately? they probably asked startled by its familiar and yet miraculous creations. Look, he says, showing her one of the photos in the catalogue. And she looked imagining herself walking in the church holding the hand of her daughter dressed in a shirt printed with a coloured map of the estuary. The two, he is sure, could have also noticed the smell, at times sweet but mostly sharp and pungent, and like others puzzled if it came from the canvases, or from the river meandering just paces away from the church or from them. And they also heard sounds ebbing and flowing in the church and some would have felt floating with the tides, in and out and up and down. Sounds interspersed with mundane noises: of the

dockyard clock, the New Year fireworks, the drunken revellers, and finally the crescendo of the dawn chorus. In the spring of that year the estuary consecrated the church by its presence, and the city and the people who frequented the church to celebrate and mourn or to find crumbs of peace would have wondered if the land on which they endured their happy and unhappy lives was fashioned by the estuary that sliced through the chalk and clay valleys, terraces, and salty marshlands. Hal(e)lu-Yah, Praise the Lord, his mind whispers. Hal(e) ha-nahar, Praise the River, her mind itches to respond.

The Calusa Indians have passed away, deported or killed, he says, but the name they gave to the river survives. Kissimmee, she says. Yes, the long water, it means, he adds, stretching between Lake Tohoekaliga in the north and Okeechobee, in the not-that-far south, from where it feeds the everglades, which flow as if they were a river of grasslands. As always, he has photos and maps to tell the story, and the story is joyous and sad, the story of a river resisting to forego its riverness, the wholeness of its past, present and future threaded together within and beyond its meandering bends. The river of water and of the everglades curve and coil like bodies of indulgent lovers wrapped around each other's fleshy folds, their bony bumps and beguiling hollows. The Calusa treasured the bends adapting their own movements to match the supple turns of the river relying on their nimble canoes, swift but humble, to paddle up and down without perturbing the fish and the birds who accepted them as genial companions, ready to make room for each other, their life fine-tuned with the rhythmic pulses of the river. Meandering had made the river capacious, able to hold more water when the storms surged, and if the season was dry, able to store a judicious amount in oxbows, lakes, and bogs. And fecund it was, she says, because slow and patient,

it readily preserved the precious bubbles of air it had gathered. It was, he says, it certainly was, and this is why the Calusa called the river alive like a creature. Almost sentient, she says. Perhaps, he replies, in its own riverly way. How clever, she wants to add impressed by 'riverly', the word he has coined. A word that, like 'almost', she spoke and both hides and reveals their desire to break the barrier in the mind of a scientist, to challenge the omniscience of a detached observer. He will break the habit, she is confident, as will she, together or otherwise apart. Their mindscape nourished by the remnants of memories of their life in friendship with water, lakes, and rivers

•

The river is sentient, he says, because it observes and responds as living beings do to endure and flourish. And it has feelings, she says, perhaps like you and me or the crimson rosella that flies in daily for a drink from a water basin squatting in the shade of a silver wattle outside my window. Perhaps it has and expresses them, he replies, because Kissimmee grieved when engineers, smart but single-minded, decided to straighten the meandering bends and push the water into a channel guarded by dams and weirs to help it deal more easily with torrents of water unleashed by storms and tornadoes. Is this because they doubted its innate

endowment, its riverly nature? she says, amazed how easily she has embraced his words, infectious. Maybe they did, he says, either from ignorance or arrogance. And once it was uncurled, the water in Kissimmee sped as though it didn't know what to do with it, as though the main purpose of its life was merely to deliver water from one lake to another without delay or overflow. They felt bereft, the river and the water, cut off from the world the munificence of which they had created and of which they remain an inseparable part. Death came slowly to Kissimmee initiated by the loss of air for which it gasped like a creature afflicted with chronic asthma. Gradually the plants began to perish, followed by fish, and then the birds deserted the everglades. The first to vanish were the spoonbills, the deep pink of whose feathers was sorely missed by the moist marshy light. The purple of the muhly grass also faded, saddened as though by the departure of sprightly grass sparrows and their dry insect-like trill. Silence descended over and around the everglades. The water in Kissimmee also quietened as if trying to remember and relive the rhythmic beat of the Calusa canoes patting the water like the hands of affectionate parents. The river of water and the everglades mourned and waited for people to hear their sighs and groans drowned often by the noise of speedy

fishing motorboats hurtling past. Did they hear? she asks. Did they have time to listen?

I hope they did

•

They did, he says, but only after Kissimmee had waited for over forty years. The relief was delivered by the engineers who were seeking a semblance of redemption. They gathered the dirt piled near the channel and filled it, restoring the meandering bends the river had fashioned over thousands of years. Kissimmee welcomed the lost clay and sand, cleansing the grains and flakes with water that was keen to resume its chatter, recalling words it had mislaid but not forgotten. The wind joined in, ruffling the purple-headed muhly grass whispering excitedly about the snail kite gliding down to catch molluscs and take off with them in its claws with water streaking down in the early afternoon light, its striped wings unfurling, celebrating with each flap the bounty of the everglades. That must have made Kissimmee jealous, she says. Maybe it did, like most siblings often feel, he replies, but it knew that it shared with the everglades the fingerprints of each other's being. Similar to genes, she says, encoded with memories of deep and distant past and messages for their future yet to be shaped. Including the scars of traumas, he says after a pause, weighing each word in his mind, because a river once maimed doesn't

quite heal, the wholeness remains impaired glaring at the world like an eyesore, similar to the remnants of the straightened channel upstream and downstream of the restored meanders. A wounded Kissimmee reminds me of my aunt who used to walk with a limp begotten from polio when she was a child. Like Kissimmee she was a river too, a river of songs and stories, of love and grace, of joys smudged with sorrows. Why was? she wonders but doesn't ask preferring instead to wait for the right moment. Will it arrive? It will, she hopes, cleaving open a slit in his troubled mind, a blurred photograph that shows as much as shrouds. Like water in a river, she imagines him say, layer upon layer

playing hide and seek with light.

Tell me about the ear, he asks. It's the ear he, perhaps naively, believes that largely made us the sapiens we are, for without hearing, speaking is impossible. From an ocean of noises, the ear and hearing shape the stream of words and speech, music and songs, calligraphy and writing. A few days pass before she gathers her thoughts to show and tell the tale of the sapien ear, a contraption that nature had conjured after several episodes of trial-and-error, negotiating umpteen bends, diversions, and false turns. There is no scientist as versatile as nature and no artist as imaginative, for nature did hit upon an almost perfect solution with traces of missteps and failures either erased or yet to be uncovered. It would have been nice, she says, to encounter nature's errors, the freakish beings, to admire and to learn about its dogged perseverance. Alas, she says, emitting the sound dampened with a sigh and they notice how it becomes a word,

salient with meaning and value

•

What about Tiktaalik, he asks, the beautiful freak? It isn't a freak, she objects, but a creature, almost flawless, that as you surely know lived longer than we, the sapiens, will ever. Unlike us it was suitably equipped to exist in harmony with the world the nature had found for it; it was happy in the water like a fish and didn't shirk spending time

on the dry land breathing air which had less oxygen than we require. Tiktaalik, he repeats the Inuit word a few times, and feels how it twirls and twines in his mouth like the rough seed of a peach. There is a bit of Tiktaalik in all of us, she says, and points at one of the three bones in the middle ear of humans in the image. The two others come from the jawbones of reptiles, isn't it? he says with a smile impish but not impolite and quietens so that she can continue unhindered. We may think and imagine that we are the pinnacle of evolution, she says, but we are assembled from bits and pieces of our ancestors from the deepest past and from the outermost regions of the earth and beyond. We are, we are, he wants to say but doesn't because to listen is his intention, and to listen with purpose without missing a word spoken by her, each word imbued with pleasure and conviction. I would love to be her child, he imagines, but tosses away the alluring thought to allow the words to enter his ears and titillate his mind and heart, the subsidiaries of the brain, nature's most judicious but enigmatic creation

•

The magic, she says, happens in the cochlea, the innermost ear, where the waves of sound change into signals that the brain and its twin, the mind, turn into meaningful words threaded together as speech. Shaped

like a snail the cochlea is filled with gel sprouted with hairs which quiver when touched and tickled by sonic waves. Like the lateral line of hair cells on the fish, he wants to say, but doesn't opting instead to hear from her the words he expects to emerge soon, and they follow without delay or distraction. The hairs in the cochlea, she says, are arranged like strings in a harp, able to generate vibrations from sounds entering the ear. Like fish we feel the sound as touch before we hear it. To hear, therefore, is to be caressed by sounds, which ride along crests and dips of breath exhaled by the speaker. How fascinating, his mind nudges him, pleased by the image it creates because it leads him to another much more intriguing than the first. Each time she speaks, and I hear, her breath flows in me like streams in an oxbow lake, and my restless mind

accepts her presence as benediction

•

Speech is a river of breath, she says, confident that the brief quote she had found in a book would confound and comfort him at the same time, for it will establish a confluence between rivers he has been preoccupied with and the stories he tells of them to entice her to walk with him, which she does as a willing and at times unwilling partner. Above the larynx, she says, is the chamber through which the

breath emerges orchestrated by players, one of which is the tongue, its root, hump, and tip. It moves up and down in the mouth, forward and backward, altering the size of the chamber, and sounds appear, soft or hard, loud or quiet, clear or muffled. Lips and nose join in to add colour and texture, timbre and tenor, and words so familiar otherwise sound afresh intoned by the mind and, some would say, heart of the speaker. Who is the conductor of the orchestra? he wants to ask but doesn't, because the answer seems obvious and yet obscure, when words we speak and hear come to us already spoken and heard by others. They arise from the ocean of speech, the source of all languages diverse but also similar, for they are fashioned by the breath we exhale. Yes, she says, but it happens only because the sapiens had acquired the skill to breathe, speak, swallow and gulp without choking. We exhale more when we speak, taking far less time on quick short breaths inhaled by us. We are nature's brilliant invention, the result of its tinkering, its playful indulgence. We are, he says, and perhaps this is the reason we can't forego the urge to question, explore and wonder about the origin of nature including our own. Are we the inevitable outcome of its grand design or just the result of chance or accident? Nothing is ever perfect or finished,

he says, which is the source of sadness and joy we inevitably feel and express. Not even a meandering river, she asks with a cheeky smile because once again she has succeeded to pre-empt his thought, waiting to find words he could have spoken, and she would have heard.

I have brought you a present, she doesn't say but hands him his smartphone and earpods. It's the river, he says after a brief pause. One of the first few words he has spoken, quiet but clear, after emerging from the fog of oblivion caused by the stroke. He listens and looks in her direction with a shy grin trying to hide the vagueness which plagues his mind forcing him to doubt if she is really sitting on a chair near the hospital bed. She is here, she is here, his mind nudges urging his hand to reach her wishing to be touched and she touches allowing the faint tremors to flow through her, and muffled sounds from the earpod that has slid from his right ear onto the pillow dowse and besiege her. She picks the pod and inserts it in her ear and the two hear together the river speak. Pebbles, he mutters. Moss and grass, she adds, and the two quieten to let the river talk. Everything else is trivial even the tiniest thought keen to put on the garb of words and break out like an overzealous mountain spring

•

They hear and listen the sounds of the river inside them and on the phone, streaming in their ears and in the highlands and lowlands of Lutruwita. It's a gift, she'll tell him later, from her aunt who has walked and paddled up and down the rivers in her canoe not once but again and again because a river

and its speech changes, she, her riverine aunt, believes like our own. It alters but also retains the echo of past sounds, which like words in a dictionary are layered with resonances of bygone peoples, places, and times. And the speech is polyphonic pregnant with a multitude of voices the landscape spawns; the landscape in which it came into being and to which it lends its spirit to form and reform. The river talks and the landscape listens and replies; their conversation melded and moulded like breaths of gracious lovers, resulting in a symphony that neither has a beginning nor a perceivable end

•

The language of togetherness has sounds familiar to them. They float above the watery harmony of the river; its babble, giggle, and gargle; its trickle, splash, and splosh; its furious foamy slap; its sedate breathy sigh, and its hush lulling rhythm. They hear and listen and resist uttering words describing the sound and its source scared to disrupt the flow of river-speech. Thus freed they let their bodies respond. A platypus snuffles and groans and his hand trembles. A boobook hoots and her grip on his hand tightens, and when a fish burps, they look at each other and smile. The trill of a golden warbler sends shivers down their spines; he raises his knees and their

hands move up his tingling thigh and leg. But the greatest thrill comes from the loud whistle of the whip bird. Soon the female will respond, his mind unwittingly whispers. I hope she does, her mind wishes to reply but she doesn't allow the frisky conjurer to break her inner silence. The river talks, and they and the world around it, listen and hear the language of togetherness. The blissful moments continue unabated, at least for now. Of the future they aren't anxious. It's the acute presence of the here and now that nourishes them. The rest doesn't matter. None at all

•

It does matter, the future, she thinks walking home from the hospital. It definitely does because it's the little glimpse of future that lights the path, where a speck of hope stands like his mother with an earthen lamp in her hand; the cotton wick dipped in a dollop of ghee flickers unsteady unsure enlightening her young but tired and sickly face. No, not his mother but her memory, for she knows the mother only lives on a small black and white photo she had stumbled upon as it slipped out from his wallet that she had retrieved looking for the organ donor's card, which she thought the doctors might need if his brain failed to drag itself and him out of the abyss. Saloni, his mother, died when he was three, he would tell her in the not-too-

distant-future, just learning to talk emitting words still quite unwieldy for his breath to bring under control and pronounce. Saloni and Solani: two words assembled from matching sounds with the first two vowels exchanging places but in both the same 'o' stressed demanding extra effort from his mouth and mind, and he often failed confusing the two; a confusion which still taints his fretful mind but he doesn't regret the mix-up, for it's the desire that rules: a desire to be close to the mother lost years and years ago

•

Up in the sky, his *maasi*, the younger sister of his mother replied each time he asked her about the place where his mother had gone to live. And the two gazed at the clear wintry sky, his eyes following the finger of his maasi tracing the flow of Akash Ganga, the Milky Way, the celestial river of stars amongst which he was told to believe that his mother sat in a boat following Cygnus, the swan, bright and graceful. Aren't the two lovely, his maasi, would say, and without waiting for his reply affirm, they are, they certainly are. They played the game for several years and then one day he discovered the truth, stark but lifeless. Saloni, his dead mother was cremated on one of the ghats on the eastern bank of Solani and her ashes dispersed in the river he calls my river. This

is when his maasi handed him the black-and-white photo, a gift both precious and onerous. The grieving began then and hasn't quite finished. It never does and never it should.

Lamentations
Subhash Jaireth

The words, 'speech is a river of breath' are taken from Steven Pinker's book, *The Language Instinct: How The Mind Creates Language*, (1994, London: Allen Lane, The Penguin Books), p. 161; Information about *Tiktaalik,* fossil and evolution of hearing was obtained from Neil Shubin's book, *Your Inner Fish: The Amazing History of our 375-million-year-old ancestor*, (2008, London: Allen Lane, The Penguin Books); The idea of a harp-like arrangement of hairs in the human organ Corti, the core of the cochlea comes from Michael Spitzer's *The Musical Human: A History of Life on Earth*, (2021, London: Bloomsbury Publishing London); The descriptions of the Medway Estuary and Stephen Turner's exhibition *Time & Tide* are sourced from two exhibition catalogues *Time & Tide: Tracing the Millennial Tide* and *Tide & Change*, generously mailed to me by Stephen Turner. A good description of the estuary and the exhibition can also be found in Roger Deakin's *Waterlog: A Swimmer's Journey through Britain* (2000, London, Vintage).

The idea about the importance of hearing and listening to the voice of the natural world is borrowed from Michel Serres, a French mathematician and philosopher. In the book, *The Five Senses: A Philosophy of Mingled Bodies*, he writes: 'We can neither speak nor sing without the feedback loop which guarantees the audibility of our own voice. The ear guarantees and regulates the mouth, which emits noise in part for the speaker, in part for others, who in turn guarantee other feedback loops.'

First published 2026

POETRY

ISBN: 978-1-7636009-8-0

BOOK, TYPESETTING, AND LOGO DESIGN
Mountains Brown Press

PUBLISHER
Life Before Man

Gazebo Books
PO Box 375
Summer Hill
New South Wales 2130
Australia

gazebobooks.com.au

This book was made possible thanks to Anthony Mark Day

COVER IMAGE: *Vegetable*, 2025, oil on canvas, 33 x 43 cm, © Phil Day

www.ingramcontent.com/pod-product-compliance
Lightning Source LLC
LaVergne TN
LVHW051009080826
845145LV00009B/2529

* 9 7 8 1 7 6 3 6 0 0 9 8 0 *